DOVES
KW-123

Contents

What Are Doves?—8
Are Doves For You?—16
Choosing the Bird—24
Acclimating the Dove—34
Care and Feeding—38
Behavior—50
Breeding Doves—56
Diseases—64
Dove Species—76
Index—93

Pages 2 and 3: *Doves are very gentle birds and make good house pets.* **Title page:** *The diamond dove, the smallest of all doves, has long been a favorite with a number of amateur aviculturists.* **Pages 94 and 95:** *The housing for your doves should provide ample room for its occupants.*
Photo credits: *Dr. Herbert R. Axelrod, Michael Gilroy, Michael W. Gos, Ralph Kaehler, Paul Kwast, Harry V. Lacey, Ron and Val Moat, A.J. Mobbs, H. Muller, San Diego Zoo, Vogelpark Walsrode.*

Acknowledgments

My many thanks go to Charles Taylor, Dr. A. S. Dhillon, Jim Plantenga, and Plantenga's Pet Palace in Lafayette, Indiana. Without their help, this book could never have been conceived, let alone written. Special thanks to Andrea Gos, who knows what it's like to live with a writer. Her help has been invaluable over the years; without her, this book would never have been written. It is to her that this book is dedicated.

Michael W. Gos

Distributed in the UNITED STATES by T.F.H. Publications, Inc., One T.F.H. Plaza, Neptune City, NJ 07753; in CANADA to the Pet Trade by H & L Pet Supplies Inc., 27 Kingston Crescent, Kitchener, Ontario N2B 2T6; Rolf C. Hagen Ltd., 3225 Sartelon Street, Montreal 382 Quebec; in CANADA to the Book Trade by Macmillan of Canada (A Division of Canada Publishing Corporation), 164 Commander Boulevard, Agincourt, Ontario M1S 3C7; in ENGLAND by T.F.H. Publications Limited, Cliveden House/Priors Way/Bray, Maidenhead, Berkshire SL6 2HP, England; in AUSTRALIA AND THE SOUTH PACIFIC by T.F.H. (Australia) Pty. Ltd., Box 149, Brookvale 2100 N.S.W., Australia; in NEW ZEALAND by Ross Haines & Son, Ltd., 18 Monmouth Street, Grey Lynn, Auckland 2, New Zealand; in the PHILIPPINES by Bio-Research, 5 Lippay Street, San Lorenzo Village, Makati Rizal; in SOUTH AFRICA by Multipet Pty. Ltd., 30 Turners Avenue, Durban 4001. Published by T.F.H. Publications, Inc. Manufactured in the United States of America by T.F.H. Publications, Inc.

DOVES

MICHAEL W. GOS

Although most doves are not as brightly colored as other birds kept by aviculturists, doves are popular because of their generally peaceful nature and ease of breeding in captivity. Three of the smaller-sized doves are the tambourine dove (above), the zebra dove (facing page, top), and the Galapagos dove (facing page, bottom).

What Are Doves?

Doves may be one of the most misunderstood creatures in the animal kingdom. Throughout history, man has never allowed the dove to be himself. Instead, doves have always been a symbol of something else. From Noah's adventure through the Holy Ghost and on to today's symbol of peace and gentleness, the bird has made its mark on mankind in a way that, surely, an individual of the species could never understand.

Perhaps it is this symbolism that makes a dove an attractive house pet to so many people. Many dove owners feel their pets bring charm and peacefulness to the home—and perhaps they do. Many aspects of their personalities are low-keyed and passive. Yet anyone who has taken a cage of doves by surprise knows that they at times can be far from placid.

Doves are members of the pigeon family. Their straight, soft bills, hardened at the tip only, and thick, meaty legs make them easy to tell apart from other birds. It is much more difficult to differentiate between a pigeon and a dove. The line of demarcation between the two is faint, if it exists at all. In general, the accepted difference is simply stated: doves are small pigeons. In practice, the difference is more a case of common names. If the bird is commonly called a dove, that will probably be its accepted classification. Unfortunately, there is no more scientific method available.

There are two basic groups of doves, the seed-eating doves (subfamily Columbinae) and the rare fruit-eaters (Treroninae). Almost all doves kept by hobbyists are seed-eaters. As such, they are walkers and spend a good deal of time on the ground foraging for seeds and other food matter. Such characteristics should be taken into account when choosing housing for the birds. The few members of the fruit-eating group are mostly tree dwellers and, as such, like to nest much higher than their ground-loving counterparts. The fruit-eaters' diet is also harder to imitate in captivity, which makes them more difficult to maintain in a healthy state.

The subtle beauty of this collared dove lies in its elegant shape and pleasing color.

Some claim the diamond dove (above) is the most beautiful of all doves. The mourning dove (facing page, top) is the most common member of the pigeon and dove family native to the U.S. This one has built an exceptionally sound nest for a dove, but it is still just a pile of twigs dumped on a window sill among the vines. The bleeding heart dove (facing page, bottom) received its common name because the red patch on its breast resembles a wound.

What Are Doves?

Technically, doves are extraordinary birds. They are the only birds that can drink water without tilting back their heads to swallow. The throat is constructed much like that of humans and other mammals, enabling doves to swallow without removing the beak from the water supply.

Probably the most exciting and almost unbelievable fact about doves and pigeons came from a recent discovery by scientists at Cornell University. The homing instinct was being studied with emphasis on the use of ultraviolet light and low-frequency sound. It is believed that doves can see ultraviolet light rays from the sun. But the use of low-level sound is even more exciting.

Indian ring dove, domestic pied variety.

The barred dove is small, attractive, and does very well in captivity.

Doves and pigeons possess such tremendous hearing capabilities that a bird flying over Lake Michigan can listen to waves breaking on both the Atlantic and Pacific coasts. The ear can pick up low-level sounds called infra-sounds. The human ear can detect sounds that go as low as 10 cycles per second. The ear of the pigeon or dove can hear sounds down to .05 cycles per second. That means a dove can hear a sound when a wavelength is about four miles long.

As house pets, doves can be unique additions to any family. Their antics are entertaining in a subtle way and their contributions to the family can be meaningful.

13

White-colored doves (above) have traditionally been associated with peace and love. Two caged doves (facing page) symbolize the love shared by this newly married couple.

14

Are Doves For You?

The first consideration in choosing a new pet is to decide if the family really wants a bird. If the house is extremely drafty in winter and harbors menacing cats or rowdy children, a bird may not be the best choice. If the family has decided on a bird, the dove is a viable possibility. Doves have a personality all their own and are not like any other pet. While they are hardy and make minimal demands of the owner, they possess a subtle appeal that a "special person" appreciates.

As a prospective dove owner, one must be ready to accept a few facts about the new pet in order for the relationship to work. First, your dove will never talk. Doves possess somewhere in the vicinity of a half dozen sounds. Thus, imitation of human

Blue-headed quail doves have been sharply reduced in number by deforestation and excessive hunting.

The African ring dove is distinguished by the pale pink color of its head, neck, and breast.

sounds is not possible. Nor will a dove ever perform a line of tricks like a cockatiel or a macaw. While they can be taught to sit on a finger, that will probably be the extent of the bird's repertoire.

A dove will never be colorful in appearance. If a flashy dresser is desired, stick with the tropical birds. It is safe to say that your dove's beauty will be subdued, at best. If a room filled with song is the goal, the family had better be fond of the male's cooing, because that single note will be the sound heard most of the time. There will be no budgie symphonies or canary concerts in the dove cage.

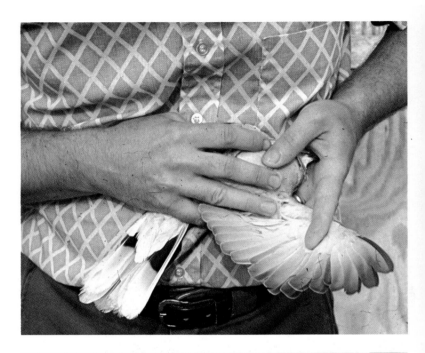

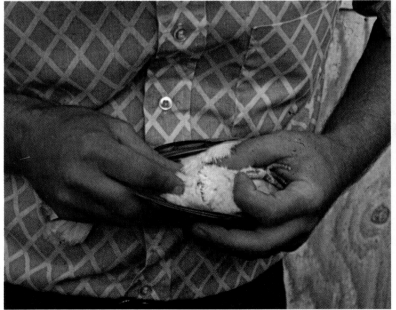

Two of the steps in picking out a bird are to examine it for external parasites (facing page, top) and fullness of breast (facing page, bottom). Of the wild doves, the pygmy ground dove (above) is one of the better choices for beginners.

But doves do have their good points. They possess a dignified charm and personality not seen in other birds. Many of the species are rather pretty, although never adorned with bright colors. For birds, they are exceptionally neat. A pair of doves can be housed in a small cage in a living room without causing the mess commonly seen around the cages of other birds.

Doves are extremely gentle. While little fingers poked into the cage may seem cause for alarm and mass hysteria, when it's all over you can be assured that the finger will remain intact.

One of the traits that makes doves such good pets is that they tend to adopt families well. Monogamous in nature, they share that devotion with their adopted human family. Once a dove has accepted the family, it will sit at members' feet or even next to a personal object belonging to one of the family whenever free to do so.

Probably the biggest plus in favor of doves as house pets is the cost factor. While some of the exotic species are quite expensive, it is not unusual to find the domestic varieties reasonably priced. For further savings, cages can be relatively small and the amount and types of food eaten will not even dent a budget. The dove is certainly one of the least expensive pets available.

A wooden dowel will make a good perch for your pet.

Facing page: *The Senegal palm dove is commonly imported, kept, and bred in captivity.*

Outdoor aviaries can be as elaborate as this battery of pens (above) or as simple as this one (facing page). The larger setup will house several dozen pairs.

An important decision to be made by the prospective dove owner is whether the bird will be used for breeding or just as a family pet. After that decision is made, you can proceed to select the dove (or doves) of your choice.

Naturally, many people think of their local pet shop as the first source for buying a dove; however, a pet shop cannot possibly stock all species of dove. If your pet shop does not carry the type of dove that you desire, you might consider contacting a breeder. It will require a little more work to find a breeder as they seldom advertise in the telephone directory, but local fanciers and pet shop owners will share that information. Additionally, you might check the classified section of your local newspaper.

The biggest problem facing a hopeful breeder of doves can be solved by the proper selection of birds in the first place. Number one on the list of breeding problems is getting the right sex. Sometimes doves are sold as pairs, when they are really two birds of the same sex.

Getting one male and one female is generally not enough. Not only are all doves monogamous, but they have a strong preference for choosing their own mates. Putting two birds of the opposite sex in the same cage is no guarantee they will ever breed. By far the best way to ensure breeding is to let the birds pair off naturally.

That is hardly practical for the new owner. Breeders, on the other hand, generally have the space and will not sell the birds until the pairing has taken place. For that reason, they should be a good source of breeding stock.

Often a single bird can be had from a breeder prior to mating, but generally all birds are kept until the pairing process is complete. As such, the pet shop could well be the only source of single birds.

Facing page: *When selecting your pet, check to see that the feathers are as clean and as evenly textured as those of this bird.*

Crested doves from Australia (facing page) thrive and multiply in this outdoor aviary. Note how branches provide natural perches. These particular birds spend the winter months indoors, but when warm weather returns, they are moved to larger, outdoor facilities. A view of the sheltered section of an outdoor aviary (above). The darker bird is a ringneck dove, the other inhabitants pied doves.

In cold climate areas, young birds may be available from breeders only in the warm months of the year, whereas a local shop can import them from other areas to provide a year 'round supply.

After choosing between buying from a dealer or from a breeder, the next choice is to select the specific breeder or shop. Price should not be a factor in this choice unless there is a dramatic difference. It has been my experience that prices in any one geographical area are not that different. When dealing with breeders, success in recent competitions, reputation, and location may all be factors. Depending on your priorities, the choice can be made. The important thing to look for is a facility that is cared for in such a way as to produce healthy birds. The same holds true for pet shops. A look at the entire bird section can tell a lot about the care the doves are receiving.

When looking at the bird section as a whole, check each bird. Do they appear healthy, happy, and well fed? Are the food troughs full? Be especially curious about food troughs of birds other than doves. Are they filled with food or just the husks of seeds eaten long ago? Examine the water troughs. Is the water clean? Are the troughs littered with droppings? Are there too many birds to the cage? Crowding not only introduces more disease, but tends generally to weaken the birds as well. If the entire section looks good, it's time to pick the bird.

Returning to the dove cages, look at the birds individually. If you have decided on a particular species or type, the decision may be made for you as there may be only one or two of that type. Should that be the case, if a healthy bird isn't available it's always better to look elsewhere until a healthy specimen is found or wait until one arrives.

Fortunately, with doves it's easy to pick a healthy bird. Before buying, do enough research to know what your chosen species looks like. Any variation is cause for suspicion. While watching the birds in the cage, observe the behavior. If they appear

The well-known mourning dove is common throughout the U.S.

dull or don't coo, something is probably wrong. Healthy doves are active. When you approach the cage, the birds should at least walk around, not just sit. They should always be on their toes when someone approaches the cage. Ideally, they will get excited and may appear hyperactive.

If possible, pick the bird up in your hands. Better still, pick up and examine each bird in the same cage. Turn each one over and inspect the vent region. If the feathers are a green color or are covered with white pastings, the bird has diarrhea. It could be a minor condition, but a novice is better off not taking the chance.

Check the feathers. Are they ruffled or have they lost their texture? Either could be a sign of problems. A scratching bird is probably infested with parasites. While handling the bird, push the feathers aside in various places and check for external parasites and mites. The bird should be clean.

The health of your birds depends a great deal on providing them with fresh food and water and keeping their quarters clean. **Above:** This is a typical water fountain. **Facing page:** Disinfectant spray is a vital part of disease prevention.

31

Now reexamine the cage. Examine the droppings on the bottom. They represent those of the bird of your choice or its cagemates. Either way, they provide an insight into the problems of the bird or of birds to which it has been exposed and from which it might have been infected. At any rate, they are an important indicator of health. Droppings should be solid. Occasionally they will be greenish and mixed with a white liquid, uric acid. In the dove's digestive system are two blind pouches called ceca. They contain the fecal matter produced by the animal and, in the healthy dove, empty twice daily. On the cage floor that translates to one dropping in five or six. A marked variation could be a sign of trouble.

Last of all, ask the shop owner how long he has had the birds. If they have been in his store less than a week, it is better to wait a few days before purchasing. One week in the shop gives the dove ample time to acclimate itself to the new location. It will need still another week to become acclimated to your home.

After you have chosen the bird, the next step is to pick out the needed accessories. If the birds are to be used for breeding, a much more elaborate setup is needed. If the bird is to be a house pet, one or two may be kept in a small cage. A good size would be two feet long by one and a half feet wide with a height of eighteen inches to two feet. Cages of this size are fine for domestic doves and a few of the smaller wild doves like diamonds, but will be unsuitable for larger birds like the Australian crested. Many fanciers who maintain several birds build cages of this size from wood and wire in clusters of four or more. Some of the more elaborate ones have special boxes built onto the ends where the birds can nest in privacy. A few of the common doves will nest in such quarters, but most of the wild ones will not.

Most doves like to walk around, and in small cages flying is not possible except in free periods when the bird is let out of the cage. As a result, there must be ample room at the bottom of the cage for the bird to walk around. It must also have a roost higher up in the cage. The bottom should have a false floor of wire mesh over a tray that can be lined with newspaper for easy cleaning. In addition to the roost, the cage should contain one large food trough and some sort of a water trough. These should be designed for easy refilling without disturbing the bird.

After the cage has been chosen, the only other immediate necessity is food. There are several different schools of thought on the proper food for doves. For now, it is important to get a supply of the food of your choice when purchasing the bird.

The best system of adding a bird to the family is one involving the purchase of the cage and other accessories prior to the selection of the dove. In that way the cage can be set up and waiting, ready to accept the new arrival. In doing so, valuable time is saved in transporting the bird from old surroundings to new. Another method would be to take the prepared cage along when picking up the bird. In that way, the bird

A pair of diamond doves.

will have more room for the trip. This is especially valuable if you intend to acclimate a young bird to periods of travel later in its life.

During the first week in his new home, the dove has plenty of new things to get accustomed to. Even if it had the recommended week or more in the shop to become acclimated to its surroundings, the new home is an entirely different environment. Privacy is the best prescription for the acclimation period. The dove must be allowed to learn its way around the cage and become used to the appearance of the room around it. This is not an appropriate time for unconfined long walks. For the first week, the new arrival should remain confined to the cage.

Because doves demand so little in the way of care, all the owner need provide is food, water, and, if there is a pair, possibly a nesting box or basket. Given those necessities, the bird will do fine.

For the next seven days the owner should attempt to keep people and animals away from the cage as much as possible. This is especially important with regard to people approaching the cage for a closer look. During this period, every effort should be made to keep the bird

from getting excited. Excitement at this point could cause a panic reaction. A head-first crash into the bars of a small cage may not be as dangerous as one in a larger aviary where the dove has been able to build up some momentum, but it certainly should be avoided nonetheless.

Another problem in the first seven days is probing by the children fascinated with the uncommon house guest. Eventually the dove will learn to take in stride fingers stuck into the cage, but for now, they will almost assuredly elicit a panic reaction that could injure the bird as it attempts to fly to safety. While new owners often get excited about the possibilities of carrying the new pet around on a finger, the urge to start right away needs to be controlled until the end of the acclimation period.

As is the case with many of the household birds, owners may choose to cover the dove cage at night. Whether this is done or not depends entirely on individual circumstances. The cover may help to stop very light night drafts if they are present. A better

The collar of this white variety of Indian ring dove is very slightly indicated as a pale band.

reason for the cover is light control. Where early rising is the practice in the household, a light turned on in a dark room can elicit a panic reaction as the bird is temporarily blinded. Thus a cover would be of some assistance.

Whatever the choice regarding covers, it should be consistent. That is, whatever you choose to do, do the same thing each and every night. Doves like order in their lives. A bird used to sleeping with a cover may wait up all night for the cover before he goes to sleep.

While most doves benefit from a free period each day where they can walk around the house, this should be bypassed during the acclimation period. A dove on the loose has a lot of exploring to do and locations of objects to learn. This is not something that should be added to his learning during the acclimation period.

Ideally, doves should be kept in the mated pairs of their choosing, but in many instances that isn't possible. If the hobbyist owns but one bird, there is no problem in housing. The difficulty often occurs with the introduction of new doves into a cage already inhabited by other birds. Many people try to add new doves to cages housing other doves or sometimes even other birds. In general, doves do not appreciate new arrivals in an established cage. It is always best to keep newcomers by themselves.

An even bigger problem occurs when doves are kept with other families of birds. While doves are generally peaceful and other birds may be also, this arrangement seldom works. Even if the birds do get along together there is a greater chance of disease developing in a mixed cage. This is especially true when doves are kept with members of the parrot family.

During the first week in the dove's new home, water should be changed daily and food checked often. Other than that, nothing should be done to disturb the bird until the acclimation period is over.

The colored feathers in the pied variety of Indian ring dove vary in size and position, but the collar is unchanged.

One premise of aviculture should always be kept in mind when discussing the care of doves or any other birds. Simply stated, all birds do better outdoors. In many cases, breeding is almost impossible indoors. However, the climate in many parts of the country does not allow year 'round outdoor maintenance of doves. While many of the doves are winter-hardy and some live in climates much like that in the Midwest, many individuals fail to make it through each winter. That is too big a risk for dove owners to take, especially with the more exotic species.

Two alternatives are to keep the birds outside during the warm months and inside in winter, or to keep them inside year 'round. For residents of Florida and other warm areas, the doves may be left outside year 'round provided they have a shelter where they can escape from rain and wind.

The first major decision that needs to be made by the new dove owner is whether or not to use a cage. For one bird or a house pet, the cage is the only way to go. Its use allows the bird to be kept in the house as a part of the family. But like so many other hobbies, aviculture can get to be habit-forming. For many people, there is no such thing as one bird. At that point, it is time to consider the aviary.

An aviary is a large pen, either indoors or out, where groups of birds are kept. Often it is just chicken wire over a wooden frame with a small open shelter in the rear. The addition of a couple of branches for perches and a box for a nest is all most birds will require. The advantages of such a setup are many. Groups of birds can become messy in the home, and the aviary keeps the problem away from the living area. Breeders need the added room to induce mating. The birds in an aviary can fly, even if only for short distances, which is a definite advantage in maintaining healthy birds. Aviaries are easy to clean. If the noise from groups of birds is disruptive of family life, the aviary can be placed away from the house.

There is no question that doves thrive better in an outdoor aviary than in a

In appearance, diamond doves are as small and as attractive as many of the popular finches.

cage. The decision must be made to the owner's advantage—what is right for you.

If your decision is to go with an outdoor aviary or an indoor one for that matter, construction is simple. Birds need flight space. Space can be saved by the use of long and narrow pens instead of square ones. A good pen size is 12 feet long and three feet wide. Several doves can be kept in each one until the pairing-off begins, at which point only one pair per pen is recommended.

Like many other birds, doves can handle cold, but drafts are deadly. For that reason, a small shelter should be located at the back of each pen. It can be as simple as a three-sided structure facing away from the prevailing winds or as complicated as a fully enclosed house with an opening for admission of the birds. Such a structure needs a large door at the bottom so it can be cleaned periodically. The bird entrance should be at flight level. For most doves, shoulder to eye level of the owner will do.

The structure of the cage itself should be either chicken wire for the smaller species or woven wire mounted over a creosoted wooden frame for the larger ones. A branch stuck through the wiring in the corner allows plenty of perch space in a natural manner.

There has been much discussion of the merits of concrete versus dirt floors. Concrete is relatively easy to hose down for a quick cleaning and is the superior floor for indoor aviaries. Outdoors, it's hard to beat the natural earth floor. Cost alone is a big factor. The weather takes care of droppings in all but overcrowded aviaries, and the natural base seems to be preferred by doves.

Virtually all successful breeders use the aviary, both indoors and out. The cost is relatively low and the ease of construction makes it viable for almost everyone. Many of this country's successful dove breeders have two sets of aviaries, one indoors and one outdoors. In cold climates that seems to be the main ingredient for success.

In addition to the health and convenience benefits of keeping the birds

Barred ground doves (Geopelia striata).

outdoors, there is an ornamental benefit as well. Birds kept outdoors have brighter colors and more attractive sheens.

Regardless of whether the dove owner chooses indoor or outdoor pens, aviaries, or cages, cleaning chores eventually become a consideration. Thus there is another plus in favor of outdoor facilities. Because of their size and exposure to the elements, they seldom need cleaning. It is not uncommon for breeders to clean outdoor pens only once a year, just before moving the birds outside for the summer. Indoor aviaries need to be cleaned a little more often; each time, of course, the pen is emptied of birds first. Cages for house birds should be cleaned twice a week. In doing so, the wire floor should always be brushed clean. The common wire brush found in most hardware stores does the job well.

All cagebirds benefit from a periodic disinfecting of all objects in the cage. The process is relatively simple, even for large-scale breeders. Regardless of housing,

The black-naped fruit dove is noted for its vivid colors.

food and water bowls should be cleaned monthly by soaking them in a solution of liquid laundry bleach and water to a concentration of four ounces of bleach to the gallon. For lightly soiled accessories, the concentration can be as little as two ounces per gallon. The purpose of this procedure is mainly to disinfect the food and water dishes. The bleach solution can kill most of the harmful bacteria, thereby preventing introduction of disease in the birds.

This hygienic practice should be taken a step further, though less frequently. Cage walls, floors and roofs should be periodically sprayed with a garden sprayer filled with the bleach solution. Small indoor cages can be either soaked or sprayed, whichever is convenient. Obviously, the inhabitants of the cage should be elsewhere when the spraying takes place.

The full clean-up should consist of cleaning of accessories, hosing down the pens, and using disinfectant sprays. In most cases that is all that is necessary for health maintenance of even the most delicate doves.

In choosing roommates for the new quarters, several facts about doves should be kept in mind. First, they are basically monogamous. As a result, pairs should be kept as pairs. Occasionally a new bird can be introduced to a cage after the death of the original mate, but that is the only time it is recommended. Since doves are territorial by nature, they resist any intrusion. In some species, such as the Australian crested, the territorial instinct is so strong that residents of a pen will often attack and sometimes even kill a newcomer. Most doves possess this territorial instinct to some degree. That makes the introduction of new birds to the established pen very difficult.

In general, doves molt in July or August. A loss of feathers at that time of year is no reason for alarm. In addition, baby doves will molt their initial set of feathers several weeks after birth. After that, they will settle to the once-yearly pattern. A marked loss of feathers at

If properly cared for, your pet can live a healthy, happy life.

any other time can be reason for concern and should be looked into. Feather loss is usually the first sign of persecution. Should the new dove become the victim of the other birds in a cage, the signs could be vague. Unless you actually see the attack, it's hard to tell when a bird is being persecuted. For that reason, fallen feathers at unusual times should not be ignored.

It can sometimes be difficult for the novice to determine when an outdoor-housed dove should be moved indoors, for either the night (in the case of caged doves) or for the winter. One sure sign of discomfort is fluffed feathers. If you notice that your bird is suddenly twice its normal size, it is safe to assume the feathers are fluffed for added warmth. Fluffing causes the feathers to lie differently, thereby trapping more air in the coat and creating better insulation. This is a sure sign that the bird is cold. Most individuals that can do so will enter their shelter for warmth in moderately cool weather. A caged house bird has no such facility and should be moved in for the night.

Generally, the caged bird is kept in a room where people spend a good deal of time. After all, the purpose of getting the bird in the first place was family enjoyment. The dove will adapt to the people in the room on a regular basis and be very comfortable or even happy when its "family" is around. In the case of large parties and the like, the dove may become uncomfortable with the large number of people around its cage. The solution is to take the cage and place it in a less crowded room. While that type of move can be a problem for some birds, the dove will do just fine.

One of the best things an owner can do for his caged dove is to give it a daily free period. Each day, for 30 minutes to an hour, the bird should be let out of his cage to go for a walk. Most doves—and all the domestic varieties— are seed-eaters and, therefore, ground-dwellers. They like to walk around a great deal. A small cage affords very little possibility for such excursions. On his free periods, allow the dove to travel around the house at will. During the hour the dove will probably leave a dropping or two, but these should be of no concern. Dove droppings do not stick to carpeting or leave stains. The benefits gained by the bird and the pleasure derived by the family are worth the minor inconvenience.

In the wild, most doves eat whatever seeds and insects are found on the forest floor. In captivity many different diets are

Check your dove regularly for external parasites.

advocated. Breeders generally prefer more elaborate diets than do owners of house pets.

Some breeders advocate a mixture of mostly millet and canary seed for the small doves and wheat, kibbled corn, and sorghum with peas or rice for the larger birds.

More convenience-oriented breeders often use a wild bird seed mixed with chicken laying mash. There are even those who advocate straight laying mash. While the chicken feed is generally recognized by experts as the best overall food for doves, many doves do not like the food and will eat it only as a last resort.

A natural perch is fine, as long as it hasn't been chemically treated.

Probably the most common food used by breeders is the commercially prepared game bird chows. A typical example is the 22% protein game bird crumbles marketed by several manufacturers.

If doves were given their option, they would take a selection of whole grains. This seems to be the choice of many house pet owners as well.

Doves enjoy a variety of foods, including seeds.

Commercial parakeet feed seems to be the mainstay of most house dove diets. When supplemented with grit and with vitamins in the water, it provides a good diet for most doves. Its convenience is also a factor for many owners: parakeet food is available in all pet shops. Game bird crumbles can often be difficult to locate, especially in cities.

As a treat, virtually all doves like well soaked dog biscuits and mealworms. Both are healthy foods for the birds and will be appreciated whenever offered.

From the owner's point of view, doves have a rather convenient way of eating when compared to parakeets. A classic problem with novice parakeet owners is starvation. A parakeet takes the husks off the seeds and leaves them in the food bowl. Uninformed owners then check the bowl, see the husks, and assume that the bird has food. Often this is not the

Bar-tailed cuckoo doves. The female's underparts are barred with blackish-brown.

case, and the bird rapidly enters a starvation state; as a result, many die. Such is not the case with doves. The seeds are eaten husks and all. It is easy to judge just how much food the bird has.

There are only a couple of "don'ts" where feeding of doves is concerned. Grit should never be mixed in

THE BAR-TAILED CUCKOO-DOVE—*MACROPYGIA TUSALLI*
1⅓ Nat. Size—Male on right, female on left

with the food. The birds prefer to take grit at their desire and do not like to have to rummage through it to find bits of food. Also, a problem can occur similar to the one for parakeets. With food and grit mixed, it is easy to misjudge how much food the bird has available, and that could eventually lead to starvation.

A favorite food of many doves is the slurry. A slurry is a mixture of food, particularly mashes, with water. While there is nothing wrong in the food itself and many doves love it, it can produce problems. The moist food begins growing fungus almost immediately. The fungus can cause a serious disease, aspergillosis. The problem can be avoided easily while still allowing your bird the treat of an occasional slurry. Give the bird sufficient time to eat and then remove the food. Do not allow it to sit and become a fungal culture which the bird will later ingest.

A dove makes a charming small pet for the right household.

As in all other areas, the dove is relatively undemanding when it comes to feeding. A few precautions beforehand will keep the bird healthy and happy for years.

Behavior

Doves tend to have characteristic behavior unlike that of any other of the common hobby birds. As mentioned earlier, they do not possess the repertoire of tricks that cockatiels sometimes display, but they can have a charm of their own, especially if teamed with the right owner.

In the wild, doves tend to be monogamous. As long as their mate is present, the breeding process will continue, weather permitting. If one partner should die, the survivor will generally pick a new mate quickly.

Doves in the wild tend to flock. Some species do it seasonally and others do it year 'round. The most usual way of seeing wild doves is in groups of six to ten hopping around the ground together. Flight is generally limited to stretches of 100 to 500 feet at a time.

Nesting, like intelligence, is not the dove's strong point. There are very few doves that can build an adequate nest. As a result, they tend to choose places with a firm foundation to help compensate for a shaky nest. In America, the common mourning dove is more likely to nest on a window sill than in a tree, and with good cause. In most species of doves the nest is simply a haphazard collection of a few twigs piled together to resemble a nest. In the Midwest, the nesting expertise, or lack of it, of the mourning dove gave us the phrase "dumb as a dove," which was an expression popular with pioneer women.

When doves do nest in trees, they do so only in a very low location. The seed-eating doves seldom nest more than 30 feet up. The fruit-eaters are much more adept at arboreal life and tend to build better nests at higher altitudes.

One characteristic noted in all species is the cooing of the male. The sound does not begin until the bird has reached maturity and is noticeably depressed or lacking female companionship. Used mainly as a courting gesture, the birds will often use it not only on the lady dove, but also on members of the adopted family. While purely sexual in nature, it is a habit that

Facing page: *The silver mutation is one of the earliest to have appeared in the Indian ring dove.*

endears the birds to their owners.

One thing doves have in common with many other birds is an occasional problem in the breeding process. Sometimes the male will kill his mate. Occasionally it is the other way around. Either instance is rarer in doves than in most other birds, but it does occur nonetheless.

Diamond doves are kept and bred in aviaries all over the world.

In the home, the caged dove tends to exhibit a slightly different personality. Domesticated doves especially seem to like human contact. Even wild doves are much more peaceful than other birds of comparable size. They tend to be as unobtrusive as lovebirds, yet their presence can add a tranquil charm to any room. Doves are very neat birds and, as a result, can be placed anywhere in the house without concern.

The golden heart dove derives its name from the deep golden yellow feathers on the center of its breast.

Probably the most important characteristic behavior pattern is their love of people. A family pet will not only seek the attention of its family, but will also accept strangers in stride. Occasionally they will overdo it in getting the family's attention. It is not unusual for a dove to begin cooing frantically as soon as it hears someone entering a previously empty house. It cannot see who it is and probably doesn't care, it just wants company.

If the avian ham succeeds in getting attention and someone goes near the cage, the dove will want to be let out immediately and often will carry on in the hope of achieving his goal. If it should succeed and be let loose, one of two things will usually happen. Either the bird will sit as close as possible to the foot of the person or it will locate some personal object, such as a lady's purse, and sit next to it. Once settled, a long, low cooing begins. Although sexually induced, to the observer it appears to be a sign of contentment or love.

Most small-scale hobbyists have domesticated doves as pets, usually ringnecks, whites, or pieds. When a hobbyist decides to acquire one of the wild types, a problem often occurs. Things don't go as well as planned and the wild dove is quickly branded temperamental. It is important to note that there are differences among the domesticated doves and even between individuals of a mated pair. It is only logical that there would be even wider differences among wild and domesticated species.

A wild species will not respond to captive conditions in the same way as does a domesticated bird, especially if the bird was born in the wild. This may never pose a problem if the doves are being kept as house pets, but breeding is an entirely different story. If that is your goal, only patience and understanding will gain you the ultimate reward. Doves are only temperamental when mishandled. Persistence in working toward an understanding of the bird will guarantee success. When the problems are finally corrected, the doves will respond.

Facing page: *This bird, the Australian crested, is best left to the more experienced aviculturist. It can be quarrelsome toward weaker doves and temperamental in breeding.*

Breeding Doves

Breeding doves or any other animals purely for profit is always the wrong approach. Nevertheless, a good breeder can do well financially with doves. Most hobbyists, however, have less grandiose aims when it comes to breeding these birds. The task of inducing breeding can range from being very simple in the case of domestics to nearly impossible in the case of some of the rare species. Fortunately, there are a few tricks that a breeder can play to increase his output once he finds the breeding pair that is willing to cooperate.

In the wild, doves generally lay two eggs at a time, but occasionally only one is produced. Generally both eggs hatch. In their early days the young are fed by a milky liquid called crop milk secreted by both parents. Young doves are very small, poorly feathered, and generally helpless. They will stay in the nest until well developed. At that time the parents begin to teach the fundamentals of flight, generally with little initial success. Characteristically, the young venture from the nest in an attempt to mimic the parents in flight. The family is usually reunited on the ground under the nest after the crash, and the parents then stay with the young until they learn to fly. After the clutch is raised, the process begins again.

In domestication, many of the habits are the same, but the intelligent breeder can make up for many of the doves' shortcomings. In the wild, it is hardly unusual for a pair of doves to lay their eggs on a bare concrete ledge and then wonder why they fall. Some mourning doves don't even bother to build a nest before breeding, the eggs being laid almost anywhere, even amidst the vines covering a window ledge. Needless to say, such habits reduce the dove population markedly. The breeder can counter this by providing a small wicker basket for the birds to nest in. In many cases the birds will drop in a twig or two and decide the "nest" looks good enough and begin laying the clutch. With the basket, the eggs have a reasonable chance.

Occasionally, in the wild one member of the pair,

For breeding, these diamond doves have been provided with a typical pigeon's nest, only it is smaller in size.

usually the male, will kill the other during mating. The breeder can watch out for these mismatches and remove one of the birds before irreparable damage is done. There is then the chance for a better pairing later.

In captivity, many doves refuse to tend the eggs once the clutch is laid. Conditions are not right for them and they abandon their nests. Fortunately, the breeder can use foster parents to hatch and raise the family. The foster family never realizes that the strange-looking young are of another species.

Immediately after weaning the first set of young, most doves will begin another clutch. For most species that translates to a new family every six weeks. Fostering allows the rarer species to breed more often since they naturally begin again once they realize the old clutch is missing.

How then does the prospective breeder go about multiplying his numbers? That varies according to the bird of his choice. For the domestic birds (ringnecks, pieds, and whites), just providing food, water, and a nesting

basket will do the job. Some of the wild types are a little more tricky.

The biggest problem facing any potential breeder is getting a pair— or more specifically, getting the right sexes. It has been our experience that doves are often sold as pairs when they actually are not. This is a particular problem when the birds sold are actually too young to be paired. An experienced breeder may be able to help you.

Once the pair is established, it is best to keep them in a cage or pen to themselves and, if possible, in the same cage all year 'round. For house birds or Florida breeders, that is no problem. In cold-climate areas, a decision has to be made between consistency of surroundings and outdoor maintenance during warm months. It is hardly a difficult decision, as breeding possibilities are greatly enhanced in outdoor aviaries.

When breeding is imminent, the male begins an almost constant cooing, generally starting at the nest. If that doesn't work, he'll go out to the female and try to herd her into the

Mourning doves are hardy and easy to keep.

nest, while cooing all the while. In most pairs, the male will be the first to sit on the nest. He will sit on it and coo until the female gets the idea. Once the ritual begins, breeding will take place within a few days. Sometimes eggs will be produced in as few as three days.

If for some reason the pair seems reluctant to breed, they could be bothered by a lack of privacy. A cloth applied to the outside of the cage will give them the sense of privacy that they seek and still allow good air flow and afford the keeper visibility from other parts of the cage area.

Once the eggs are laid, the ritual process of setting and hatching begins. Setting on the eggs is a joint effort in doves. In general, the female sets on the eggs at night, the male in the daytime. In some species a phenomenon called doubling is common. Just prior to hatching, both birds will crowd onto the nest and set together. There has been some conjecture that the parents may be able to feel stirrings in the egg and are thus cued to the imminent arrival. However, there have been incidents of doubling noted at what appeared to be the hatching time of clear eggs. That suggests that doubling is probably done in response to some sort of biological clock rather than the feeling of stirring within the egg.

Once the eggs are

hatched, both the parents produce crop milk to feed the young. They are very attentive to the young up to the point of weaning. The breeder interested in producing young doves would do well to remove the young once they are weaned and allow the parents to get back to business without outside distractions.

Groups of weaned doves can be kept in a pen together throughout the summer. After the first molt (baby molt), the maturation process begins. By the time the birds reach the summer molting period, they are about ready for pairing. Allowing each bird to pick its own mate will give better results with breeding attempts in the future. If at all possible, young doves should be kept by the breeder until the fall so that mated pairs can be established before sale. The value of mated pairs may not show up financially, but it will show in the reputation the breeder builds for himself. Even if it is possible to determine that you have two birds of the opposite sex, putting them together does not work as well as letting them pair naturally.

The best way to establish pairings seems to be banding in a group cage. The procedure is to put four or five birds into one pen. Each bird is move them to a pen of their own. It is imperative that paired birds be removed promptly. Allowing them to stay in the community cage almost always precipitates

marked with a different color leg band and the birds are then allowed to pair off naturally. Regular checking of the cages will show the pairs as they form. A mated pair will quickly sequester themselves in a corner and try to establish territorial rights and gain privacy for breeding. By noting the color of the bands on the birds, the breeder can then go in, pick out the pair, and

In the wild, most doves are principally seed eaters.

fighting. Once the pairing has occurred, there is a very high probability of success with breeding. Nevertheless, the pair should be watched in case they happen to be that rare pair where one will attempt to kill the other.

One breeder, who is probably characteristic of many dove breeders, raises Australian crested doves for marketing. This fairly rare species is rather expensive, and he can sell all he can produce at a rather handsome price. His birds produce a clutch of one or two, hatch them, raise them, and then begin again. The problem is that, since he lives in a cold climate, the birds breed only during warm months. That leaves him with two clutches per year, maybe three if he's lucky. Through a process called fostering, he is able to stretch that number to 12 or 15 times yearly.

Fostering is the raising of a clutch by birds other than the biological parents. Because doves will accept other birds' eggs, this possibility has grown into standard practice among breeders. In this case, there are several pairs of ringneck doves and pieds laying eggs. A good ringneck will bring the breeder only a nominal price per bird. To the commercial breeder, then, baby ringnecks are virtually worthless. Whites and pieds are not worth much more. In this case, the Australian crested doves lay eggs, and in the meantime, so do the

ringnecks. The breeder then takes the eggs as soon as the clutch is laid and puts them in the ringneck nest, while disposing of the ringneck eggs. While the less expensive birds raise the first clutch of cresteds, the parent cresteds are busy laying another set after finding the first set gone. In this way a new clutch can be produced weekly and six clutches can be raised in the time that used to be required for one.

In practice, the requirements for fostering are simple. First, the eggs should be roughly comparable in both species. Placing a chicken egg under a tiny diamond dove would not produce good results. For larger doves, whites, ringnecks, and pieds are the best birds for fostering. The young of smaller species can successfully be fostered by diamond doves. Second, the foster parents must have laid a clutch of their own to accept the foreign eggs. Third, the timing should be close. The eggs need to be taken from the biological parents right after they are laid. If the foster parents have already been sitting on their eggs for two weeks, it is highly unlikely that they will stay on the new eggs long enough to hatch them out.

There is another type of fostering that can be of assistance to the breeder in emergency situations. Occasionally one or both parents will take ill or die during the rearing process. Since they are then incapable of caring for the young, something must be done. In the past, the young were written off as lost. Recently, however, there have been reports of a different type of fostering, that of young already hatched. The babies are placed with a new setting female. It has worked with birds that have just laid their own clutch as well as with birds raising hatchlings. The new birds will often adopt the young as their own and care for them. Later, should the original parents recover, the young can be placed back with them. Since the sick bird has gone to hospital quarters, she is unaware that the young were moved and will accept them immediately. This, of course, depends on the young having been

Be sure your dove doesn't have access to poisonous trees or shrubs.

put into the nest just prior to the return of the adult bird.

While not the most natural of processes, fostering can add to a breeder's success without turning his aviaries into a baby factory. In this case it is used to save lives that would otherwise be lost.

Diseases

Fortunately, doves are extremely hardy birds, probably the hardiest in the aviary. But even the hardy birds occasionally turn up sick. Twenty years ago there were considerably more problems with doves than there are now. Many of the old problems are unheard of today. One reason could be that the depression and World War II brought a rash of people raising doves for squabs. With food as the only incentive, little study was done on the birds, and living conditions for them were poor. Now the dove population is less widespread but much healthier.

There are still a few common diseases that veterinarians see regularly. By "common" we mean that they show up often in the doctor's office. No disease is truly "common" in the dove population as a whole.

Without a doubt, the most common complaint that dove owners have with their birds is diarrhea. If it were a disease in itself, it would be the predominant one. However, diarrhea is merely a symptom of several different problems. Before assuming the worst, a wise move would be to think about the weather to which the ailing bird has been exposed. Diarrhea can be caused by long and continued exposure to damp conditions, particularly in cool weather. If that cause is suspected, a few days of being kept warm and dry should solve the problem. If not, a visit to a veterinarian is recommended.

Cool, damp weather can also cause colds in doves. A cold in a dove is as minor as one in his owner. The bird should be kept warm and dry and watched to be sure pneumonia does not develop. Some of the older literature advocates a few drops of glycerine be added to the drinking water as a tonic.

A rare problem in doves is constipation. It is also one difficult to detect unless the bird is in a cage by itself. Older literature recommends tepid olive oil taken internally as a remedy. An easier solution

Facing page: *Proper care and a good diet will help keep your bird as healthy looking as this one.*

A pair of diamond doves (left) ready to begin the nesting process. A pair of crested quail doves (below) in the act of mating. While no baby birds (facing page, top) are beautiful, squabs seem to be more attractive than most. This mourning dove will brood hers until they are ready to leave the nest. Production (facing page, bottom) may be increased by hatching eggs in incubators.

would be the feeding of laxative food.

Occasionally, when a bird is taken by surprise or extremely frightened, it will appear to be having a fit. The best solution is to try to calm the bird while keeping it cool. Most birds respond well to being placed on their back in the owner's hands. A very light rubbing of the chest tends to calm the bird immediately.

If a cold should progress to the point of becoming pneumonia, the bird will probably be in serious trouble. Depending on how early the disease is caught, the veterinarian may be able to help. Again, there is no substitute for regular observation in determining when there is a problem.

In addition to the above, doves seem to be susceptible to most diseases that affect chickens. Three diseases causing diarrhea that are better known in chickens are *E. coli* infections, coccidiosis, and salmonella infections. Generally, the amateur bird fancier will not be able to diagnose or treat any of these without instructions from a veterinarian. It is important to note that

while veterinary care can be expensive, especially for birds, it will never be as expensive as replacing an aviary full of birds once the disease hits epidemic proportions.

It is also important for the dove hobbyist to remember that while most doves find slurries a real treat, these goodies should never be allowed to remain in the cage more than an hour. As soon as they are mixed, slurries are a great culture medium for molds and other fungi. When left in the cage overnight, as is frequently the case, large amounts of fungi are present. When the bird eats some of the leftovers, it ingests these "cultures." The end result is a disease called aspergillosis. In addition to causing internal problems, this disease can also infect the eyes and in extreme cases can cause blindness.

Another group of diseases to which doves are susceptible is parrot diseases. This transference will occur when the doves are kept in close proximity to members of the parrot family. The most dangerous of these

When surrounded by foliage, the crested dove may be difficult to see.

diseases is psittacosis. Its claim to fame is the fact that it can spread to humans. Another parrot disease is scaly-leg. The ailment is common to all parrots and parakeets and spreads to doves. Tiny mites invade the scaly parts of the leg, causing irritation.

Since bird diseases are extremely hard for the layman to diagnose, the

Dimorphism makes cape doves (left) easy to sex. Not so the ringnecks, exemplified here by the African ring (below) and pied dove (facing page).

best that can generally be done is to tell when the bird is ill. The following symptoms indicate a problem in doves. Most of them are applicable to other birds as well. The bird:

1. is quiet (abnormally so);
2. has ruffled feathers;
3. behaves abnormally (generally quieter, but can be anything);
4. carries its head to one side;
5. has balance problems;
6. sits a lot rather than stands; or
7. exhibits changes in color or type of droppings.

Should any of the above symptoms occur, it is highly recommended that a veterinarian be consulted. It can sometimes be difficult to find a doctor experienced with birds, but it is necessary and should be done before the need arises.

Most bird diseases are difficult to diagnose, even for professional breeders, and even the common diseases are tough. Very few fanciers can differentiate between lice and mites, for instance. As such, a veterinarian's

diagnosis is vital.

As with any animal, including the human variety, prevention is the key. Providing the proper housing and shelter is a big step in the right direction. The regular bleach spray is another plus. Skipping either step is a calculated risk. Sooner or later, the fancier and the doves both come up losers.

Veterinarians are called in often to treat injured birds. With most minor injuries, professional assistance is not necessary. All the owner needs to be aware of is the chance of infection. Watching for problems and responding with the proper treatment keep the problem minor. Of course, some major injuries require medical attention and should be so treated.

Given the proper care, there should be little need for medical help during the life of a normal dove. However, when such development does occur, prompt action can prevent massive problems later.

The bar-tailed cuckoo dove is distinguished by its very long tail.

Grouped with the ring doves as "turtle doves" are species that include the European turtle dove (above) and the palm turtle, or laughing, dove (facing page).

No introductory book could ever cover all the varied domesticated and wild species of doves. Many scientists believe we still have not discovered all the different species. By its very nature, this book will cover only those commonly kept by hobbyists. If further information is sought on specific species, there are several books available and several of the bird magazines carry more current information on the individual species in articles written by hobbyists like yourself. Such information is often the best available on the subject since it relates directly to small-scale raising. For the beginner, there are two basic classifications of house doves: domesticated and wild. Occasionally a species will straddle both categories as is the case of the diamond dove from Australia. In the text that follows, those species will be treated that are domesticated.

DOMESTICATED SPECIES

Ringneck Dove The most common house pet of the doves is the ringneck. Actually, it is believed that there are seven different species of ring doves and the most common is said to be the Barbary dove. Some of the birds commonly found in the hobby trace their ancestry back to eastern Europe and North Africa. Ringnecks are by far the least expensive doves to purchase and the hardiest. Commercial breeders like them because they are excellent foster parents for the larger wild types such as the Australian crested. The bird is generally a faded brown color and has a ring of deep brown to black circling three-quarters of the neck and open in the front. The color is less intense than that in wild doves, as is the case with most of the domestic types. Generally, doves found in pet stores are ringnecks or whites. The coo in ringnecks is unusually loud, as is the laughing sound they make. In addition to the domestic varieties, there are several wild varieties possessing

Facing page: *A male black-naped fruit dove. The female of this species is green and does not have contrasting head markings.*

The crested quail dove (above), native to Jamaica, is now well established in captivity. Ruddy ground doves (facing page, top) have been frequently imported from their native Mexico and South America. Peruvian ground doves (facing page, bottom), sometimes called gold-billed ground doves, are widely kept in American aviaries; these small doves are easy to maintain and breed.

slightly different characteristics. Ringnecks are members of the group commonly called turtle doves, a group that provides all domesticated species commonly kept in the hobby.

White Dove Throughout history, this dove is the one that has received all the press. From Noah's time to the time of recent peace negotiations, the white dove manages to get involved in one way or another. Its origin is less clear; some say it is a species unto itself, while others claim it is a mutant of the ringneck. Either way, it has all the main points of the ringneck except color. The white is just that: solid white from beak to tail. The white is seen in many breeding operations as well since it is also a good foster parent. While a little more expensive than the ringneck, the price is generally moderate in range.

Pied Dove Like the whites, the pied is thought to be a mutant of the ringneck. Many people consider this bird the least attractive of the domestic doves. With a white base covered with splotches of brown to gray, the pied looks like an artist's rendition that never got it together. It too has all the other traits of the ringneck. All ringneck-type doves share a trait that makes them perfect for the beginner: they can be kept in small cages, with no apparent problems. Even large parakeet cages will do in most cases, and the birds will often even breed in such small quarters.

Diamond Dove This bird still exists in the wild, but is so commonly bred that much of its population in America can now be called domesticated. Like the ringneck, the diamond dove is a member of the turtle group. Many people consider them to be the most beautiful of all doves. They are considerably smaller than the ringneck, since they are the smallest of all doves. The gray and brown color is set off by small dots of white on each wing. The eye is circled with orange. The eye ring is a reliable determinant of sex in this species, the ring being much larger in males. As a result, the diamond is one of the few doves that is

The diamond dove, attractive and hardy, is a favorite of amateur hobbyists.

easy to sex. The ring size does not differ, however, until after the second molt, so a dove would be reaching six months or more in age before sex could be determined. The diamonds are probably the best choice for the average beginner for many reasons. They are smaller and require less space, are much prettier, and are nearly as hardy as the ringneck. In addition, they can be easily kept with other peaceful birds, particularly the larger finches. Many bird fanciers who find doves too dull and uninteresting to devote a cage or pen to them can add a diamond

Fruit doves are very colorful birds, but, perhaps because of their requirements, only a few of the species that have been imported have gone on to breed in captivity. Pictured on this page are an orange-fronted fruit dove (left) and a black-naped fruit dove (below). The spotted turtle dove from Asia (right) is likely to do well in warm climates.

or two to a cage of the much more attractive finches, and they will display nicely.

FOREIGN WILD TYPES

While there are many hearty and beautiful wild doves, they cannot be as highly recommended for a beginner in the hobby as the domestic varieties. While the average beginner will probably have success, neither the birds nor the hobbyist need the headaches that such a pairing will cause.

The beginner trying to keep wild doves will often find them temperamental, especially when breeding is the main purpose. Of course, as is the case with most animals, the problems are in mishandling by the keeper rather than in the personality of the birds. Persons attempting to keep wild doves should be aware of the kinds of problems they are likely to encounter and the conditions required by the particular species of their choice. Given those warnings, many suitable pets can be found among the following.

Australian Crested The Australian crested, named for its native habitat and headgear, is about the size of a ringneck. A little temperamental in breeding, even for the experienced aviculturalist, they are nevertheless easy to keep. While attractive in their own way, they do not compare with the diamond doves for looks. Beginners trying to breed this bird are often in for several surprises. They demand more privacy than many birds and occasionally they fight among the pair, sometimes to the death of one partner. Prices of the birds are often prohibitive, and finding specimens is difficult. Hobbyists should keep in mind that smaller species, like the diamond, can be comfortable in a moderately sized cage; but a larger type, like the Australian crested, will need more room.

Cape Dove Cape doves are about the size of diamond doves and make a good starter bird for those new to wild types. For a dove, the bird is quick in all movements and possesses a unique ability to hover over a given point. It is easy to tame and is

The crested quail dove spends a good deal of time on the ground foraging for food.

generally a calm, quiet bird. They breed freely. The young are easy to rear, with the only problems occurring if the babies leave the nest too soon. In spite of their North African origin, they are very cold-hardy and can be kept year 'round in unheated aviaries.

Pygmy Dove The pygmy is one of the best wild types for beginners and is roughly the size of the Australian diamond dove. Its short tail causes it to look much smaller. While there are several races of the bird native to Central and South America, virtually all of them make excellent pets. They are relatively easy to maintain and breed.

Of the larger-sized doves, the bar-shouldered dove (facing page) has a reputation for easy breeding. Bartlett's bleeding heart dove, also called Bartlett's pigeon (above), shown here sunbathing, is well known in captivity, though only a few have bred.

Dwarf Turtle Dove This is the only turtle dove in which the sexes can be readily told apart. The male is mostly gray as opposed to the female's brown color. Not recommended for cages, the dwarf turtles do exceptionally well in aviaries. Since they are hardy and breed easily, they are a popular bird for many serious hobbyists.

Spotted Turtle Dove This Asian bird is fairly common with hobbyists in the warmer sections of the country. An attractive little bird, the spotted turtle dove does well in an aviary with its own species or mixed with other non-violent birds.

Tambourine Dove The tambourine dove is one of the more popular wild types in the hobby. Named for the rather unusual coo they produce, like the sound of a tambourine, these little birds are rapidly becoming common in the U.S. While they are not imported heavily, they do breed fairly easily. The parents are effective in rearing the young. When the ten-day-old bird falls out of the nest, the parents join him on the ground for another seven to ten days. Tambourines are not cold-hardy and need some heat in cold climates. A pile of straw or hay under the nest improves the chances for survival of the young when they fall to the ground. This is one of the doves that is easily sexed. The male's underside is a pure white, compared to the gray color in the female. In addition to seeds, tambourines also eat insects and snails in the wild and should be offered live mealworms regularly for best health.

Galapagos Dove These little doves, named for the islands of their origin, make fairly good aviary birds. They are very tame and easy to sex. The male is considerably larger than the female. They are best kept with their own species as they tend to be quarrelsome. They require slightly different breeding conditions than most doves, since they nest among rocks. Recessed areas made of rocks or wood are helpful in the breeding cages. Some breeders report that after a few generations there is a problem of sterility among Galapagos doves.

**Peruvian Ground
Dove** Probably the most
attractive and adaptable of
the small wild doves, this
South American bird is
well known for its unusual
coo. Peruvians are not only
extremely hardy, but they
also are very animated for
doves. That quality
sometimes makes them
inappropriate for housing
with other small doves. In
this species, males and
females are easily
differentiable by color. It is
recommended that
Peruvians be kept only in
aviaries as they tend to be
too active for cages.

Blue Ground Dove The
hobbyist who fails to see
the difference in sexes in
this bird is blind. So
distinct are the male and
female that they are often
mistaken for different
species. The male is a
steel blue compared to the
dark brown of the female.
Blue ground doves are
hardy and always do well
in captivity. Because of
their peaceful nature, they
can be kept with most
other peaceful species.
Breeding is fairly simple,
and the young rear well.

Ruddy Quail Dove The
ruddy is one of a number
of quail doves and is so
named for both its color
and resemblance to a
quail. Quail doves are a
little more difficult to feed
than the doves previously
listed, so the hobbyist
should determine if the
inconvenience is worth the
pleasure of having them.
Quail doves should be fed
some animal food in
addition to the regular
seed or crumbles diet.
Small bits of raw meat or
water-soaked animal
biscuits will do, but grubs,
worms, and insects are far
superior. All the quail
doves are cold-fragile and
need to spend cold winters
in a heated aviary. The
ruddy stays close to the
ground, nesting in the
smallest trees close to the
forest floor. If kept warm
and given the proper diet,
the ruddy quail dove does
very well in captivity.

**Blue-Headed Quail
Dove** One of the more
beautiful doves, the blue-
headed quail dove is
generally found in the
rapidly deteriorating
forests of Cuba. Trapping
for its excellent meat and
deforestation have made
this bird rare in the wild. If

Scaly doves (left), imported from Brazil, acclimate well and breed easily in captivity. This view of a white dove (below) emphasizes the need of doves for plenty of grit. This mourning dove (facing page) has appropriated a weaver's nest.

startled, this species prefers to run away rather than fly. It is very quick afoot, so most of its time is spent on the ground. Generally, the only time this bird goes into the air is to roost at night. As a result, a pen with a good amount of floor space is advisable. Sexing is difficult, although in mated pairs the female is generally the smaller of the two. Grubs should supplement the diet if possible. Other soft food will do should grubs be unavailable. Like all quail doves, the blue-headed needs heat to survive in the cold months. Frost must not be allowed to form.

NATIVE DOVES

Mourning Dove Since the ruthless destruction of the passenger pigeon, the mourning dove is the most common member of the dove and pigeon family in America. Found in every state in the summer and in 40 in the winter, the mourning dove is a familiar species to most people in this country. For this reason it is not as popular as many of the other birds kept in the hobby.

Although fairly attractive with their brown and white markings and extremely winter-hardy, mourning doves do not seem to take to cage life well, so a pen is usually required. Check local game laws before attempting to collect a specimen from the wild.

Inca Dove These little doves are common in the southwestern U.S. and thrive in captivity. Like the mourning dove, their familiarity has caused them to be less popular in the hobby.

Passerine Ground Dove These are very common in the south but local laws regarding their capture should be checked prior to collection. This tiny dove is found virtually everywhere in its range.

FRUIT DOVES

There are several species of fruit doves that may catch the eye of the beginning hobbyist. They are probably the most beautiful members of the pigeon and dove family. The problem is that feeding, living conditions, and the like can be difficult to provide unless they are kept in a large greenhouse.

Index

Acclimation period, 34
Aspergillosis, 68
Australian crested, 84
Aviary, 38
Basic groups, 8
Behavior, 28, 50
Blue ground dove, 89
Blue-headed quail dove, 89
Breeding, 56
Breeding stock, 24
Cages, 20, 32, 41
Cape dove, 84
Care, 38
Ceca, 32
Coccidiosis, 68
Constipation, 64
Cooing, 50, 58
Crop milk, 56
Crowding, 28
Diamond dove, 80
Diarrhea, 29, 64
Diets, 44
Digestive system, 32
Diseases, 64–72
Domesticated species, 76
Domestication, 56
Doubling, 60
Drafts, 40
Dwarf turtle dove, 88
Feeding, 38
Food, 34
Fostering, 58, 62
Fruit doves, 92
Fruit-eaters, 8
Galapagos dove, 88

Grit, 48
Grubs, 92
Hearing capabilities, 13
Homing instinct, 12
Inca dove, 92
Lice, 72
Mated pairs, 36
Mites, 29, 72
Molt, 60
Mourning dove, 92
Nesting, 50
Nesting box, 34, 36
Pairing, 24
Parasites, 29
Passerine ground dove, 92
Perches, 38
Personality, 16
Peruvian ground dove, 89
Pied dove, 80
Psittacosis, 69
Pygmy dove, 85
Ringneck dove, 76
Ruddy quail dove, 89
Salmonella infections, 68
Scaly-leg, 69
Seed-eaters, 8
Selection, 24
Slurry, 49
Spotted turtle dove, 88
Tambourine dove, 88
Tree dwellers, 8
Water, 34
White dove, 80
Wild doves, 84

DOVES
KW-123